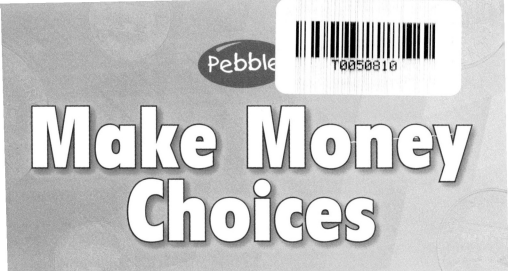

Pebble

Make Money Choices

by Mary Reina

Consulting Editor: Gail Saunders-Smith, PhD

Consultant: Dr. Sharon M. Danes
Professor, Family Social Science Department
University of Minnesota

CAPSTONE PRESS
a capstone imprint

Pebble Books are published by Capstone Press,
1710 Roe Crest Drive, North Mankato, Minnesota 56003
www.capstonepub.com

Library of Congress Cataloging-in-Publication Data
Reina, Mary.
Make money choices / by Mary Reina.
pages cm. — (Pebble books. Money and you)
Audience: K to Grade 3.
Includes bibliographical references and index.
Summary: "Introduces young readers to different money choices and discusses needs
versus wants"— Provided by publisher.
ISBN 978-1-4914-2082-9 (library binding)
ISBN 978-1-4914-2300-4 (paperback)
ISBN 978-1-4914-2304-2 (eBook PDF)
1. Money—Juvenile literature. I. Title.
HG221.R344 2014
332.024—dc23   2014022152

Editorial Credits
Michelle Hasselius, editor; Kazuko Collins, designer;
Gina Kammer, media researcher; Kathy McColley, production specialist

Photo Credits
Glow Images: Hill Street Studios, 10; iStockphotos: bowdenimages, 18; Shutterstock: Andresr,
cover, 6, Jaren Jai Wicklund, 14, michaeljung, 12, Monkey Business Images, 4, Sergey Novikov,
8, Tejus Shah, 16, wong sze yuen, 20
Design Elements: Shutterstock: elic (background), kavalenkava volha (coin)

Note to Parents and Teachers

The Money and You set supports national social studies standards related to production,
distribution, and consumption. This book describes and illustrates money choices. The
images support early readers in understanding the text. The repetition of words and
phrases helps early readers learn new words. This book also introduces early readers to
subject-specific vocabulary words, which are defined in the Glossary section. Early readers
may need assistance to read some words and to use the Table of Contents, Glossary,
Read More, Internet Sites, and Index sections in the book.

Table of Contents

Name Some Money Choices

We choose how to use our money. Spending, saving, and donating are all money choices. What choices will you make?

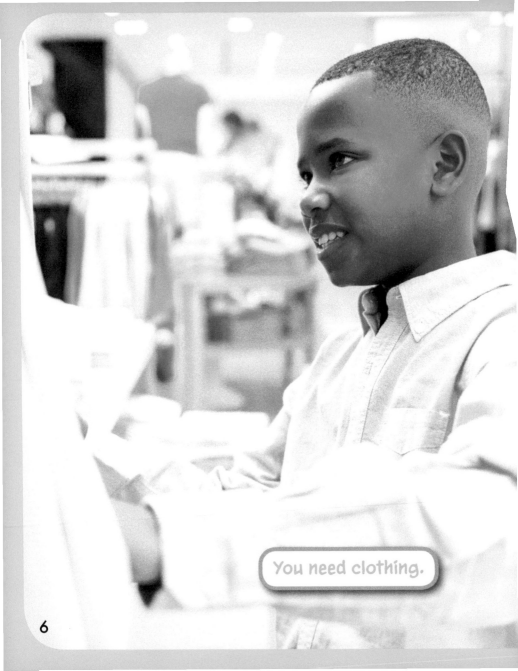

You need clothing.

You spend money to buy things you need. Needs are things you must have. Food, a place to live, and clothing are some needs.

You can also buy things you want. Wants are nice but you can live without them. Toys, video games, and candy are wants.

Choosing Between Needs and Wants

David can have candy or a piece of fruit as a snack. He wants candy. But David needs fruit to stay healthy. He picks the fruit.

It can be hard to tell needs and wants apart. Kathy is shopping for shoes with her mom. She wants the same kind of sneakers her friends have.

You need a warm jacket and boots in the winter.

Kathy's mom says her winter boots are too small. Kathy needs boots to keep her feet warm. Maybe she can get the sneakers another time.

More Money Choices

Money can be saved. Kathy puts some of her allowance in a jar every week. Soon she'll have enough money to buy the shoes she wants.

Your parents can help you find places to donate in your area.

Kathy and David donate some of their money. They buy cupcakes at a school bake sale. The money they spend helps the school buy items it needs.

Making good money choices teaches you to use money wisely. You won't waste money. Then you can keep more of the money you earn.

Glossary

choice—picking from several things

donate—to give something to help others

earn—to receive payment for working

need—something you have to have; food, clothing, and a place to live are needs

save—to keep money to use later

spend—to use money to buy items

want—to feel you would like to have something; you may want a new bike or a snack

Read More

Moore, Elizabeth. *Wants or Needs.* Wonder Readers. Mankato, Minn.: Capstone Press, 2012.

Rau, Dana Meachen. *Spending Money.* Money and Banks. New York: Gareth Stevens Pub., 2010.

Schneider, Christine. *Lily Learns About Wants and Needs.* Money Basics. Minneapolis: Millbrook Books, 2014.

Internet Sites

FactHound offers a safe, fun way to find Internet sites related to this book. All of the sites on FactHound have been researched by our staff.

Here's all you do:
Visit *www.facthound.com*
Type in this code: 9781491420829

Check out projects, games and lots more at
www.capstonekids.com

Critical Thinking Using the Common Core

1. One money choice is to donate your money. What does donating mean? (Craft and Structure)

2. It can be hard to tell needs and wants apart. Give an example of a want and a need. (Key Ideas and Details)

Index

Word Count: 223
Grade: 1
Early-Intervention Level: 19